The China Cabinet and other poems
仙人柜及其它诗

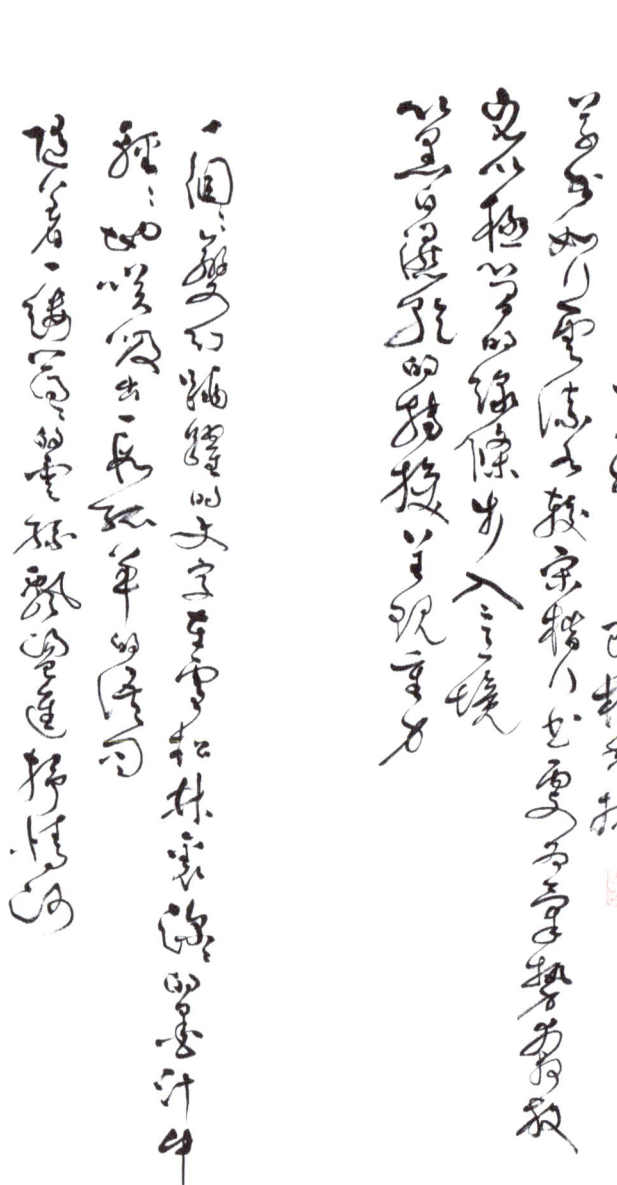

Christopher Nailer

The China Cabinet

and other poems

仙人柜及其它诗

translated by

Alice Ayres
He Wenhui
Connie Pan
Annie Ren

Acknowledgements

Working on this collection has been a true collaboration. I have been fortunate to work with four wonderful translators who have added depth to the poems.

The beautiful *cao*-style calligraphy of 'Calligraphy' on the frontispiece is by my respected teacher Paul Hsiu Pa Yang. Photography and digital imaging of the calligraphy is by David Beach.

Many Chinese friends have helped with comments and suggestions along the way.

Several of the poems were published before in *Blundstones and a Brown Dog* (Ginninderra Press, 2006).

Cover design by Agnes.

The lines in italics in 'Miss Qu Takes Entrepreneurship' come from David Hawkes's translation *Ch'u Tz'u – The Songs of the South*, originally published by Oxford University Press, 1959, republished by Penguin Books, 1985 © David Hawkes, 1959, 1985, reproduced here with permission.

The China Cabinet and other poems
ISBN 978 1 76041 820 5
Copyright © Christopher Nailer 2019

First published 2019 by
Ginninderra Press
PO Box 3461 Port Adelaide 5015
www.ginninderrapress.com.au

Contents

The China Cabinet	8
仙人柜赋	9
Translation in Beijing	10
译于北京	11
Calligraphy	12
草書	13
No Pinkerton	14
并非平克顿	15
The Department	18
中文系	19
Uncompleted – hexagram sixty-four	20
六十四卦 火水未濟	21
My mother made gardens	22
我母亲营造的花园	23
Long March jacket	26
长征夹克	27
Bicycle rickshaw, Chengdu	28
成都的三轮车	29
Market gardens, Kew	30
基尤，市场菜园	31
Dining alone by faulty street light, Beijing	32
北京，故障路灯下独自晚餐	33
Decline and fall	34
衰亡	35
Chicken scratches	36
鸡爪印记	37
Red lacquer wine cup	38
红漆酒杯	39
Oracle bone	40
甲骨	41
Qu Yuan in a Beijing bookshop	42
屈原在北京书店	43
A message from the Chairman	44
主席的指示	45

New steam age	46
蒸汽机的新时代	47
The pig truck, Beijing	48
北京的饲料车	49
Three ways	50
三种道路	51
Paul Lin at TopCom	52
顶电有限公司的林保罗	53
Tiananmen	54
天安门	55
'Uraly'	56
'Uraly'	57
Miss Qu takes Entrepreneurship	58
屈同学上创业管理课	59
Members of the China Cabinet	62

These poems are dedicated to the memory of Arthur Waley,
who inspired generations with the beauty of Chinese poetry,
and to Stephen Lee, whose teaching opened the way.

The China Cabinet

The carved elmwood doors tell the story:
a lady on the terrace by the jujube tree,
her long sleeve trailing, reaches shyly to the
zigzag railing; a gentleman pauses at the door,
his fan peremptory, the child in the upper storey
seems to call out – they don't see the fairies in
the flying phoenix or hear the zithers;
Almost a mirror-image on the other panel:
two gentlemen search the night with a lantern,
a young woman upstairs – they don't hear the
Lord and Maiden of Everlasting Life bearing down…
And it's the china cabinet stuffed with treasures
unpacked from boxes after the last move:
In the top half, the good white plates, a Japanese
teapot set, some fine illustrated cups, Helen's
trousseau collection of wafer-thin cake plates in
Shelley's Dubarry pattern, the best cutlery, two
Thai teak salad bowls, a Peter Rabbit porringer,
family silver coffee spoons and four others by
Georg Jensen that we bought in Denmark, a
stoneware dish by someone no longer a friend,
a heavy Greek olive tray, and the steam iron with
its cord curled up – for the cabinet stands closest
to the power point – circular lint brush, ditto;
And down below, the last willow pattern plate
from a broken set and the best glasses carefully
boxed in their original cardboard…
And all heavy with stories no one ever hears.
The fairies and the phoenix, the Lord of Long Life,
have sung over marital hoards many time before:
They know there is no 'later', no special guests;
these need to be used, broken, lost, given away, set free…
Let the doors swing open, let the beauty fly abroad!

仙人柜赋

榆木门上的雕饰诉说着故事:
阁楼上的女子,长袖飘盈
含羞倚着栏杆,垂眼望枣树;
男子在门口停下脚步,
倨傲地摇着扇,楼中的孩童
仿佛在呼喊——他们看不见
凤凰身后的仙人,也听不见琴声;
另一边,彷佛镜里的倒影
两名长须男子
在黑夜中提着灯笼,
还有阁楼上的年轻女人
他们也听不见——长生不老的神仙
纵身而越的声音……
这不过就是个仙人柜——摆着些
搬家后从纸箱里拆封开来的玩意儿:
上半层,有不错的白色瓷碟,
一套日本茶具,几只精致花纹杯子,
以及海伦的嫁妆——印着皇家锦绣纹样
薄如蛋壳的雪莱糕点碟,还有上好的餐具,
两只泰国柚木沙拉碗,一只彼得兔浅口碗,
祖传的银质咖啡勺,外加四支
我们在丹麦买的名牌勺子,
一个不再是朋友的人做的粗陶盘子,
一只笨重的希腊橄榄碟,和一个被电源线缠绕着的
蒸汽熨斗——只因为仙人柜离电源插头最近
同样原因,还放这个圆形去毛球器;
下半层,有从一整套中
仅存下来的一个青柳纹餐盘,
和小心地装在原包装盒里的
最好的酒杯……
这些玩意个个都背负着不为人知的故事。
仙人、凤凰、长寿之神们,
在婚姻的囤积之间多次传唱:
没有"以后",也没有贵客;
这些需要被使用、损坏、丢失、赠送……
敞开大门吧,让美好的事物飞出!

HW & AR

Translation in Beijing

for Arthur Waley

You never came here, never thought it necessary to
add the smells and sounds, preferred it ascetic,
intellectual, better to gauge the subtleties of sense, of
vanished tenses, the violence of delicate conventions,
hopes and lusts, strictures of time and place abstracted,
as one might today read Beowulf or Mallory –
does one really need to see the axe blade fall?

Thus each word carries weight, carefully chosen for
its blindness to the waste of faith, the famines,
the burst levees, bombings and the rush to revolution,
Jewish-Ottoman intaglios de-puzzled into clean
sprung rhythms of Hopkins and the Bloomsbury set.
The rules were strict and simple: Never question
the promises of beauty. Read carefully. Get it right.

译于北京

致亚瑟·威利

你从未来过这里,从未想过要沾染
这里的气息和声音,你偏爱以隐士
和学者的方式,去揣摩文字里的深意:
消失的时态,优美语法的束缚,
欲望和希冀,时间的限制,地点的遗失,
正如今日再读《贝奥武夫》和马洛礼
是否需要亲眼看见斧刃落起?

每个字都如此沉重,小心翼翼地选择
为了避而不见,信仰的抛弃,
轰炸、饥荒、决堤,和匆匆奔赴的革命。
犹太奥斯曼的铜版画,被解读为
霍普金斯风格和布卢姆茨伯里派别
诗歌里整齐的跳韵。规则严格而简单:
从不质疑美的承诺。仔细阅读。从不出错。

HW & AR

Calligraphy

for Paul Yang

Cursive
is more than
Song orthography
running
it's the
minimal character of
meaning
dynamics of
black and white
wet and dry
weight and
power

a
magic dance
of text
softly breathing
deep charcoal
from the
cedar forest
under thin cirrus
the flow of a
single sentence
down the
lyric river

草書

草書　　　贈楊秀拔

草書如行雲流水，較宋楷行書更為氣勢奔放

它以極簡的線條步入意境

以黑白濕乾的轉換呈現重力

一個個變幻跳躍的文字，在雪松林裏深深的墨汁中

輕輕地嘆吸出一段孤單的語句

隨着一縷薄薄的雲絲飄盪進抒情河

AA & CP

No Pinkerton

General Williams was no Pinkerton,
there's no shadow of doubt:
plying his Ballarat gold fountain pen
against Chinese immigration,
Commonwealth Representative for
aid to the Empire of Japan after
the Great Kantō 'quake of '23.
Did he shop for kimono in between
official engagements? Or for an
eggshell-thin coffee service,
or for two oil paper parasols, or a
wooden toy Chinese junk?
He admired the modern Japs,
industrious little chaps: silk top hats,
morning coats, wing collars,
Prussian uniforms, quite different
from the Chinese; there's a lengthy
correspondence with Morrison on
the subject, and about a likely war.
And the year after Mukden
Japanoiserie, the current mode,
swept his daughter-in-law aboard
the SS *Nankin* to Shanghai and
Yokohama. So maybe they were hers,
souvenirs for the sister at home
with her four-year-old, for the
brother-in-law mad about boats?
Or was he sentimental after all,
forgetting he'd lost his wife?
There's the kimono now, splayed
like a red-black specimen on
my mother's wall: no one ever
wore it. And the other things,

并非平克顿

威廉将军并非平克顿
这是无需置疑的：
他用家乡特制的黄金钢笔
驱逐中国移民，
在1923年关东大地震后
当选联邦代表
赴日进行支援
他是否在官方事务之余
购得一套和服？或是一组
薄如蛋壳的咖啡杯，
又或是两把油纸伞，
还或是一支中式木帆船？
他欣赏日本人，摩登而勤奋，
戴着丝绸礼帽，穿着晨礼服，翼型领，
普鲁士蓝的制服，
和中国人很不同——
他长期与北京的莫理循通信，
讨论过那一场潜在的战争。
奉天会战后的一年，
他的小姨怀着对日本文化的憧憬，
登上了南京号轮船，
经由上海抵达横滨。
或许那些纪念品是她的
买给家乡的姐姐
和她四岁的侄子，
以及痴迷帆船的姐夫？
还是他终究柔情，
忘了妻子已逝？
如今那件和服，
像一只黑红的蝴蝶标本
悄悄地伏在我母亲的墙上
从未被人穿过。
还有其它的纪念品

dusty in Grandfather's house with
their mysteries for later. The boy
poked his fingers through the
last brittle webs of the parasols,
tried sailing the wooden junk
in the bath, watched as the precious
coffee service was brought out for
special guests, little thinking of
the questions they left hanging.

带着自己的秘密
静静躺在祖父房子的尘埃里
等待有一天被发现——
小男孩的指尖穿过
残破的油纸伞,
他试过让木帆船在浴缸里航行,
他看过精美的咖啡杯被拿出来
端给尊贵的客人。却从没想过
那些纪念品背后的故事。

HW & AR

平克顿是意大利作曲家普契尼创作的歌剧《蝴蝶夫人》中的男主角。故事讲述1904年驻守日本的美国军官平克顿与一位日本艺妓蝴蝶的爱情故事

威廉将军(1855 - 1943)是作者的曾外祖父,也是《泰晤士报》驻北京的特约记者莫理循(1862-1920)的好友。威廉将军曾任墨尔本西本部地区《巴拉瑞特邮报》的总编辑。

The Department

Intimate, incestuous almost, odd bedfellows –
Maoists, spooks and dreamers –
captives to Cold War orientalism
by languages and character –
fantizi, jiantizi –
Confucius and the Party Daily side-by-side,
proses with a jolly good Oxbridge ring,
essays from May Fourth aching with unworldly youth –
and underneath, the Greats – Mencius, Sima Qian,
Du Fu, Guan Hanqing, Cao Xueqin –
unforgettable foundations.

Across the desks each morning, a litter of glossaries,
close focus for getting it even halfway right,
heads together over hundreds of pages of text,
days in a blur…

For there was a girl, so beautiful and fair,
the hours a weather vane of her presence/absence,
night-time Chinatown innocent as dictionaries,
an ancient poetry timid and undeclared –
times little short of dying.
But the world turned away beyond all reason,
decades of journeys intervening,
till she – unvariably lovely – called suddenly from China,
Singapore's monsoon lowering a screen for these old movies,
all the characters so alive.

中文系

亲密无间、几近狎昵、同床异梦的友人
毛派、间谍、梦想家
冷战时期东方学影响下
语言和文字的俘虏——
繁體字，简体字
论语和党报并读，
带有牛津英语风格的散文翻译，
透着不谙世事痛楚的五四杂文
追根溯源，重温经典——孟子、司马迁、
杜甫、关汉卿、曹雪芹——
伟大的的奠基人。

每天清晨的课桌上，一堆词汇表
努力，就算只能答对一半，
埋头，在这数百页的文献，
岁月模糊地逝去……

仍记得彼时佳人，美丽窈窕
她的出现与缺席牵动人心
夜晚的中国城，像书本一样纯洁
犹如古诗般拘谨而含蓄——
光阴过客，逝者如斯，
没有逻辑道理可寻，
几十年的路途走过，
直至她忽从中国致电——从未改变的亲切。
新加坡季风降下如帘的雨，投映着黑白老电影
主角们鲜活如初。

HW & AR

Uncompleted – hexagram sixty-four

Kang Xi coins answer bronzed out
success hinted new spring's thawing
little fox skips halfway over thin ice

fire over	water if
fine men	yield to
premature	lightness

it furthers to cross the great water
reed banks shuffle uneasy edges
caution or precipitate tail-wetting

no blame	abysmal
after rain	attackers
breaking	persevere

cart-halt humiliates deliberation
humble mastery closes off remorse
harvest wine fully three years turning

unripe yet	the ready
discipline	demands
anonymous	promises

六十四卦 火水未濟

康熙銅錢內尋其所解
終得讖語曰雪融春近
小狐汔濟之輕躍薄冰

火居上　　　水居下
君子也　　　慎辨物
其之暉　　　吉之光

征凶未濟將利涉大川
葦岸冰融也水波蕭瑟
謹慎而進之或則濡尾

坎之上　　　無可咎
雨作後　　　寇者至
攻克之　　　知其極

揭車亦羞也其之有意
賢德有善則心無祇悔
有酒而飲之需足三年

花無果　　　事未濟
以其律　　　得所願
隱姓名　　　而志行

　　　　　　　　　　　　　　HW & AR

My mother made gardens

My mother made gardens
in every house we lived in growing up;
after the army, the last one Japanese,
of washed stones and pearl white gravel
from the sparkling shallows at Warburton,
heaved into place around a dugout pond,
my father's one attempt at concreting.

She planted it with small azaleas,
a cherry tree, russet red maples, and in
the pond itself, water lilies opening
their pink and ivory throats to the
hum of hover-flies in summer,
cast iron lanterns with candles for effect.

Chinese miniatures in platters were the
prototype, done on the kitchen table
at her father's house, waiting
for a home of her own; a piece of
broken mirror for the pond,
sand around it, pebbles, moss for the
mountain with its pottery pagoda,

glossy green like the glazed temple on
Xiang Shan, a half-moon china bridge
and a bearded old man sitting
dangling a minute fish from thread
tied to a toothpick – I met him later
in the works of Liu Zongyuan –

我母亲营造的花园

年少时代住过的每一个家,
都有母亲亲手营造的花园;
最后的日式花园,是父亲退伍后,
用来自沃伯顿晶莹透彻的浅滩上
被水冲洗过的硕石和珍珠白卵石,
铺垫环绕成的一个人工池塘,
这是父亲唯一一次使用混凝土。

母亲在园内种植小杜鹃花,
樱桃树,红褐色的枫树;
在池塘内种植睡莲,
它们粉红色花瓣和象牙色的花苞
在夏天的花蝇的嗡嗡声中盛开;
铸铁的蜡烛灯笼更是营造了氛围。

沙盘中的中国微景物件皆是
样板,在我外祖父家的餐桌上
做好备齐,等侯
挪进她自己的家;一块
破裂的镜子权当池塘,
沙子环绕池周边,有卵石,青苔
的山还装饰有陶瓷塔。

它光泽的绿色就像香山寺庙的
琉璃瓦,一座半月形的中国桥
和一位蓄长胡子的老人端坐著
用牙签做成的鱼竿
垂钓着一条小小的鱼——
我后来在柳宗元的诗中遇到了他。

There was a shop you could buy these
tiny things in Little Bourke Street…
But she didn't care for crippled trees –
their wired branches, clipped roots, brutal,
unnatural, the gardener's version of
bound-feet; 'When we get our house,'
she said, 'I'll plant them out.'

小柏克街的一家商店里
你能买到这些园林小物件……
但她并不喜欢那被扭曲的树冠——
捆绑的枝杈，缩剪的树根，残酷的挤压，
非自然生成，缠足般的园丁作品；
她说过，"当我们有了自己的房子，
我要让它们在大自然的土壤中茁壮成长"

AA & CP

Long March jacket

My Long March jacket, ploughed-earth brown,
wears many Chinese winter miles,
wandering museums and temple gardens,
plodding stifling subway tunnels, it
shrugs out the stark north wind howling down the streets.
It's a throwback to Mao, the fighting intellectual, or Zhu De,
the warrior with the honest soldier's grin;
It's a foreign correspondent

looking old amongst the Beijing hipsters,
their crisp cool haircuts, tight jeans and bum-freezer jackets.
But I haven't braved the warlords nor the harrying,
nor the treachery of bribed village headmen nor the
invading Japanese…
Its veteran look is completely fake.
It's drunk my sweat in my small marches, there and back.
Have we learned anything on the way?

长征夹克

翻耕泥土色的长征夹克,陪伴着我
度过了漫长中国冬天的里程,
游历了繁多博物馆和寺庙花园,
穿行过那令人窒息的地铁隧道,
抵挡过街道上凛冽呼啸的北风。
它重现了昔日善战智者毛泽东,
面带士兵憨厚笑容的战将朱德;
和那个外籍战地记者。

它与时尚的北京人格格不入,
他们都有统一的酷发型,紧身牛仔裤配搭流行短上衣。
我没有经历过军阀混战,
也没面对过受贿的伪村长
或是日本侵略者……
这退伍军人形象完全是个假象。
它在那些暂短的往返征途中浸透了我的汗水。
征程中我们又领悟了多少?

AA & CP

Bicycle rickshaw, Chengdu

We took it because, today,
taxis weren't picking up foreigners;
the next meeting was minutes away and
crucial to the client. Thus,
for what seemed ages, I sat under an
invisible pith helmet, watching
the thin blue serge of a jacket stretch,
shoulder to hip bone,
then on the alternate diagonal,
as he heaved on the pedals.
The traffic was bad, all at a standstill;
a bus driver wedged him in;
there was a shouting match:
'Anyway,
what the fuck is the "foreign guest" and
his fancy-girl getting a *lao touzi* like you
to pedal all across town for?'
She smiled, awkward, Eng. Lit. major
not interpreting this for the foreign capitalist,
in a fog of diesel fumes
within sight of the factory, where
wheat and barley and rice and corn and sorghum
steeped in pungent heaps under
hempen sacks beneath an old steel roof,
to be tossed and mashed into
pure branded white spirits,
fuel for top-class celebrations.

成都的三轮车

我们上车,只因那天
出租车不载外国客;
下场会议即将开始,
对客户来说至关重要。
时间忽然变慢,
我仿佛戴着探险帽,看着
那蓝色哔叽薄外套,随着
车夫吃力地踩着脚踏板,
从肩至胯绷紧,松懈,
松懈,绷紧。
拥堵的交通,让一切停滞;
公交车司机插到车夫前面,
引发了一场激烈的争吵:
"他妈的,这个'外国人'
和他的靓妹儿
干啥让你这老头子
拉着满城跑?"
英语文学专业的她尴尬地微笑,
不为外国资本家翻译这段对话。
在柴油的烟雾里,
隐约看见工厂,那儿
大麦、小麦、大米、玉米、高粱
披着麻布,垒成刺鼻的一堆,
在铁棚屋顶下
等待被碾压、搅碎后
酿造成盛宴的催化剂。

HW & AR

Market gardens, Kew

At the bottom of Walmer Street hill
on the flats below the footbridge
a solitary Chinaman in black rubber boots
chugged his petrol rotary hoe
down deep rich river-loam furrows

Three generations lived under
vernacular bamboo and iron
a shack approved for farm equipment only
And every few winters the Yarra quietly flooded
not the turbid gouging torrents the elders fled

In summertime the red tin shrine
wafted joss over the kindly earth
the whole family bent under bamboo hats for
cabbages, lettuces, broccoli, carrots, silver-beet

Great-grandfather walked
a hundred miles upcountry to scratch for gold
gleaned just enough for the lease here on the bend
'Gold's poison,' he said. 'It will break you.
Grow food instead.'

基尤，市场菜园

沃尔么街山坡脚下
人行桥下的河畔上
一个孤独的中国男人脚穿黑胶靴
手推油动旋转犁锄
步履蹒跚地突突开进那深厚肥沃的河泥中

祖孙三代人住在一个
用乡竹和铁件搭建的
只许可存放农具的简陋小屋
每隔几个冬天亚拉河水都会缓缓漫过河床
不同于让长者们逃逸奔命的山洪泥流

夏季辉映着红色的铁皮神龛
烛香飘荡过那片可亲的土地
全家人都头顶竹帽弓腰劳作
卷心菜，生菜，西兰花，胡萝卜，银甜菜

曾祖父曾长途跋涉
一百英里路迁徒去淘金，
历经艰辛只为凑足这菜地的租金
他说"黄金是毒药，会害死你"。
"最好种植蔬果取而代之"。

AA & CP

Dining alone by faulty street light, Beijing

Under the arcing street light you look in,
your face, my face, merge into one:
you-me, male-female, Chinese-foreign,
a composite from two sides…

there…there again…
the light translates you…

stuttering into the dark gaps,
snapshots more immediate than opera,
death-masks fused upon the window…

I put my hand to the ice-cold glass,
your breath lingers on the other side,
a thudding in my head isn't the temple's drum,
demolition walks down the neon characters.

北京，故障路灯下独自晚餐

那盏狂闪不停的路灯下，你看到了，
你的脸，我的脸，幻影重叠成一张脸：
你—我，男—女，中国人—外国人，
屋内窗外人们的阴影融合为一个人……

那里……还是那里……
光闪的变化转释了你……

闪烁进入黑暗的瞬间，
速影的转换比京剧男旦更即时，
像京剧脸谱融汇在玻璃窗上……

我举手贴在那冰冷的玻璃上，
你的呼吸仿佛萦绕到那一边，
脑海里隆隆作响声不是寺庙的鼓声，
而是拆迁物在霓虹灯下的消失声。

AA & CP

Decline and fall

You ask me why I ply these
dictionaries over the annals of
some dead forgotten king
when our daughter's here and
now needs answering.

The texts remain the same,
and barring another Chu Silk
Manuscript or more bamboo strips,
I know everything there is about
there and then:

the king's folly, the treachery,
flight from the burning capital,
the murdered children,
it's all complete…

But the circus of us here now
seems endless: this shaky
weatherboard house, this
playing out… And are we also
to decline and fall?

衰亡

你问我为何把头埋在字典里
去寻找那被遗忘的
消逝的君王的史迹
而此时此刻我们的女儿
需要我的回应。

文献千年不曾改变,
除非有新出土的
楚帛书或竹简,
我已经知道
关于彼时彼刻的全部:

君王的昏庸和群臣的叛变
从都城火光里逃离,
被谋害的孩子们,
一切完整呈现……

然而我们之间的闹剧
却似乎漫漫无期:
在风中摇晃的房子,该朝什么方向前进……
难道我们也一样
终将衰亡?

HW & AR

Chicken scratches

It was a meditation, writing them out,
line after line, page after page, day after day –
stroke order, meaning, Romanisation,
fixing them in muscle memory;
I'm overwhelmed by their neon cousins en masse
the moment I leave the airport.

And old Uncle Don, illiterate kid drover
from Renmark, joined up for excitement,
shot badly through the hip just after Gona,
would put his head in his hands after
too many beers on the back veranda and mutter,
'Jap chicken scratches. You *read* that?'

鸡爪印记

沉思冥想写出这方块文字,
一行接一行,一页又一页,日复一日——
笔画顺序,含义解译,罗马化,
正存储在肌肉记忆中;
在我离开机场的此时此刻
各色的霓虹灯众表汉字让我不堪重负。

我的唐老叔叔,伦马克的牧者
从小不识字,参军只为图热闹,
戈纳战末却被子弹打穿了胯骨,
多杯啤酒灌肚后他双手抱着头
在后阳台上愤懑低语,
"那个像鸡爪子挠痕的日本字;你也能看懂?"

AA & CP

罗马化:语言学的一个术语。在本诗中指把汉字转换成汉语拼音。

戈纳:指1942年11月至1943年1月澳美联军在新几内亚与日本军队作战的布纳·戈纳战役。

Red lacquer wine cup

for Hugh Wylie, 1942–2000,
Royal Ontario Museum

Red lacquer wine cup from the Han,
a tranquil shape perfect for
two cupped hands,
'ears' exactly where
the thumbs would rest,
'flying cloud' design, inscribed,
'Wine to prosper My Lord' –
you could almost hear the tears.

Komaba student hostel, Tokyo, 1974,
cold, hard linoleum floor,
cheap Mercian claret,
Janis Joplin on the stereo;
And he opened this art catalogue
and the narrow study flooded with
absolute perfection;
And I couldn't stop the tears.

红漆酒杯

为纪念加拿大多伦多皇家安大略博物馆
休·威利博士(1942-2000)而作

汉朝的红漆酒杯,
静谧精美的造型恰为
双手合捧,
两侧有"耳"
持耳捧杯拇指恰可放松,
"漂浮的卷纹云"环绕杯身:
"君幸酒"——书在杯中
你几乎能听到那泪滴声。

1974年,东京,驹场留学生会馆,
冰冷,坚硬的油毡地板,
廉价的南斯拉夫红酒,
伴随着詹妮斯·乔普林的摇滚乐;
他翻开了那本文物介绍
顿时那狭窄的居室浸没于
极致的完美;
我的泪水也禁不住地流淌。

AA & CP

Oracle bone

An accident
of geography: the Headmaster –
ex-Intelligence – after the War,
looking at the map, concluded
that, apart from tradition and
those truly interested in history
or the classics, Chinese made
more sense than Latin or French,
so he searched and found a very
young man to teach it. And thus
towards the end of each interview –
the new-boy and the father – the
choice was presented. And this had
to be the strangest thing on offer. So
the boy began in that diffident way
of all teenage boys – part idleness,
part showing off – and he somehow
survived the Second Form cull when
young Mr Lee rid his class of time-wasters,
and then, with nowhere to hide amongst the
remaining twelve, surprised everyone – except
the Headmaster, who had seen this sort of turnaround
before – by starting to excel. Later, at University, it
was the only thing of interest, well, apart from acting, Japanese,
motor-bikes, and the endless search for love. Thus Y. R. Chao's
text and Chomsky's generative grammar at breakfast, Lu   Xun,
Lao She and Ba Jin for lunch, and the rich fare of Mencius, Du Fu
and Sima Qian over red wine before, during, after dinner and late   into
the night. And into that select world he pitched himself. "Oh,   Chinese will
be so valuable," everyone said, "considering our geography,   trade relations,
our regional future…" But those reasons didn't call him except   in rare manic
moments of wanting to rule the world. Government service judged   him neither
an asset nor a threat – too much the intellectual, insufficiently pre   dictable, excessively
poetical. And, anyway, with the Vietnam War on, he turned his   back on it. Thus jobs
were scarce except for teaching, translating, plying a trade in   characters; and those he did
assiduously and in many places – tutoring the next generation of   students, wrangling school
kids forced into it, coaching Chinese kids in English, or at Franco's   language school teach   ing
a strange fellow who worked for Armaguard who could never quite   predict his schedule,   and
a young Aussie wife anxious to make a good impression when she   met her Malaysian   mother-
in-law; and battling every kind of text – a geological survey map, a   Hong Kong actor's   contract,
glossy brochures for marketing real-estate, texts for the Professor of   Political Science,   historical
papers on the archaeology of Qin Shihuang. And all through that, hyp   notically un   winding Chu Ci's
magical star names, flower-names, from a battery of dictionaries night   and day,   hunkered down in his
father's studio-loft, the money always tight. Japanese computer manuals came   to the rescue – yards of them –
steady work for years. For by now there was a   child… But surely there was more than   this..? And it happened
tacitly, ever so slowly,   by   other   accidents, shape-shifting from the medium,   to the message, to
the meaning, to the mar   ket,   and   quietly, strategically from intermediary to   turning the minds of others.
Thus by enduring he grew expert in endurance 'til the language disappeared. But even through   the years of everything
else it was always there. Yes, truly, in the end, it's only valuable if you absorb it into your cell-   structure, breathe it invisibly
from the pages 'til it makes your   heart leap, to live in the essence of the teaching.   As one of the Professors
said: "There's no sense or rhyme to   continuing with it unless you simply cannot help yourself."   And suddenly he's flown
there annually to walk amongst   the billion, to reach across mindsets, a watcher, a listener,   an actor on the stage,
bewildered by the audience. For   suddenly it's quite the normal thing and there are hundreds   of fluent
experts   for all   those rational   logical reasons. And suddenly from China the world is   made of
real-estate. So it's   vital to go   back into   what's been forgotten. After all, what's left   except
philosophy, via the   classics?   And French   and German and Greek too – for the   passion
needs   its own deep   culture also… If the energies hold up… And the remains of today   drift
like White   Paper folded   into the ship   of state floating the Eternal Question:
Politics   and   Pragmata?   Or Justice, Civilization, the True, the Beautiful
and the   Good?   Which way go the cracks?

甲骨

这纯属
地理上的偶然： 前情报人员，
如今的校长—— 在二战之后
看着地图总结到除了沿袭传统
和对历史及古典文化感兴趣的
学生之外学习中文比拉丁文或
法文更加有意义 于是他找到了
一位来自香港的年轻教师。
每当面试快结束时新来的男孩
和他的父亲总会被提供学习中文
的选择。对他们来说，这是个最
新奇的提议。从此那个小男孩开始学习，
带着少年的拘谨，一半出于无聊，另一半
又带些炫耀。他莫名其妙地通过了中学
二年级的选拔，年轻的李老师巧妙地摆脱了
一批浪费时间的学生男孩在剩下的十二人中
无处藏躲，他变得出色起来。这让所有人都
感到吃惊除了校长，也曾见过这样的转变。
到了大学，除了表演、日语、摩托车和不断地
寻觅爱情这是他唯一感兴趣的事。这是早饭搭配
赵元任的理论和乔姆斯基的语法，午饭享用鲁迅、
老舍和巴金，还有孟子、杜甫和司马迁组成的饕餮盛宴，
伴随着不间断的红酒从晚饭前直到深夜。在那个他投身的
领域里：每个人都是这么说"噢，中文会很有用的。要　　考虑
我们的地理位置，贸易关系和地区未来……"但他并　　不是　为了
这些理由，除了一时头脑 发热的时候——荒谬地想要　　功成名就。
政府部门认为他既没有利用价值又不构成威胁——　过于　学者，难以捉摸、
诗情满怀。而越南战争的惨烈，让他不愿意服务。于是　　工作 寥寥，除了
教书和翻译—— 在语言和文字之间游走；而那些他辛勤　　地 做过太多
教授未来的莘莘学子，训斥不愿上课的孩子，辅导中国　小孩的英文，或是在
弗朗哥语言学校给一个奇怪的男人上课他在安保物流公司　　工作 是
不能确定日期，还有一位年轻澳洲妻子，急切地想在初次　见面时讨好　　她的
马来华裔婆婆，翻译了各种各样的文体——地质测绘图、　香港演员合同，　　房地
产市场宣传资料、给政治学教授的文本、关于秦始皇的　　考古文献。与此　同时，
他深深地沉迷于《楚辞》的世界，神秘的星辰、奇异的花草，　　在山河　中徘徊的
幽冥，令他如痴如醉，日夜埋首于字典和书籍，蜷缩在父亲的阁楼里——　生活总是
捉襟见肘，幸好有堆积如山的日本电脑说明书，好几年的稳定工作。　那时他已为人父……
但这并不是　　故事的　　全部，　　一切无计划地发生着，缓慢地，甚至太过缓慢，语言
从媒介变成了　　讯息，　从讯 息化身为意义，从意义成为市场的工具。悄然地、有策略地、
旁敲侧击地改变他人思想。通过忍耐他变得擅长忍耐，直至语言看似消失可是哪怕那么多年都　　做着
无关的事，它依然那里是的，　　　　千真万确，到了最后，只有让它渗入骨髓，　视它为氧气，
贪婪的从书本里汲取，直至　　内心雀跃, 活在所学的知识里, 这才是它的价值。　　　　正如一位　　教授
所说"除非你情不自禁，否则　　继续毫无意义。"忽然间，他每年都飞去与　　十亿人　同行，接触不同的
思想。做一个旁观者、一个聆听者、　一个舞台上的表演者，观众让他感到困惑。　　忽然间，这成了
一件正常的事，出于各种合理　　的原因，诞生了语言流利的专家们。忽然间，　　　　在中国看来，
这个世界只是一个巨大的房地产　　市场。因此必要要回到那被遗忘的经典　　　　　除了那当中的
哲理，还剩　　什么足以依靠？　而法语、德语和希腊古典，亦是如此　　　　　　对文明的
热爱促使了　对自身根源的　　追寻　　如果尚存　力气……而今 残留的
一切，　像由　　白皮书叠成的　　纸船我们的命运，在永恒的疑问里沉浮：
究竟该投身政治　　还是埋头务实? 还是选择公正、文明、真理、美丽
与　　正义？　　　　甲骨上的兆纹指向何处？

HW & AR

Qu Yuan in a Beijing bookshop

Her question hard, straight to the solar-plexus:
'What's so interesting about some poet who
complains about not being listened to, then
drowns himself? China has hundreds of them.
And thousands of ordinary teachers, doctors,
engineers, really useful people, went through
much worse. They survived…?'

And I try to explain the magical flights, the
rich botanica, the dark spirits of rivers and lakes,
the frustration of the individual voice, and how,
in those times, if you lost a royal patron,
there was no way out. 'Have you read it?'
I press a *baihua* copy on her. Next day she asks,
'How do you know about Qu Yuan?'

屈原在北京书店

她的问题一针见血毫不留情:
"那恨不得志
投水而死的诗人,
到底有什么意思?中国有许多这样的人。
而那无数的普通教师、医生、
工程师,真正有用的人们,
经历过更多苦难; 却活了下来……?"

我试图解释《楚辞》中奇幻的历险,
珍花异草,山鬼河灵,
诗人的挣扎,以及
被君王贬弃在那时意味着
无路可走。"你读过吗?"
我塞给她一本白话翻译。第二天,她问:
"你是从哪儿知道屈原的?"

HW & AR

A message from the Chairman

(50th Anniversary of the People's Republic of China, 1 October 1999)

A father walks his boy over the long week's holiday,
looking in the showroom windows,
waiting, hoping.

That day the radio cracked and hissed and that voice
made the hair on people's necks stand up…

Same clips repeat in twenty colour sets:
Japanese invading over the Wall, bombing Shanghai,
the Chairman looking out from Tiananmen,

State visits, oversized armchairs,
Mao, Deng, Jiang impersonating statuary;
and even the Americans –
Nixon, Carter, Bush – look monumental;
brows of the interpreters frown history in between…

The man tips a few coins down the slot-machine;
Sprite thumps in the outlet guaranteed to fizz;
the little boy skips.

So we didn't go to war;
families still have children;
80% believe the next decade will be better;
middle class is close enough to touch it, smell it:

What happened to 'Serve the People?'

Take heart, old fellow, here's two certainties:
You'd better get him dinner before sundown;
He'll want a toy fighter jet tomorrow.

主席的指示

(1999年10月1日，中华人民共和国成立50周年)

长假的街道上，父亲牵着儿子，
盯着商店的陈列窗，
等候着，期待着。

那天广播沙沙地响起那个声音
让所有人汗毛竖起……

一排排彩色电视不断重复着几个画面：
日本入侵，炮轰上海，
毛主席从天安门城楼上眺望，

国事访问，威严的贵宾椅，
毛泽东、邓小平、江泽民，正襟危坐；
就连那些美国人——
尼克松，卡特，布什—— 神情肃穆；
历史在翻译员的皱眉中诞生……

男人在售货机里投下几枚硬币；
这里的雪碧保证嘶嘶冒气；
小男孩兴奋地跳起。

最终我们没有打仗；
孩子们仍留在家里；
百分之八十的人们相信未来会更好；
小康的日子即将来临：

说好的"为人民服务"呢？

放心吧，兄弟，有两件事可以确定：
日落前你要带他吃饭；
明天他会想要一架玩具战斗机。

HW & AR

New steam age

Stainless steel machine
transports the creative class in Xintiandi;

Stephen Sun at the handle,
twist, knock,
shovels black grit into the basket,
locks tight, opens steam cock…

Lifts warm China cup,
balances it,
black oil dripping into a small white sump;

Ready with the steel jug,
opens the valve again, tweaking,
hissing through a milk of cows;

Pours then spoons
the perfect ratio for
a cappu-Chino,
gathering momentum now…

Shanghai morning's murder without the
Orient Espresso.

蒸汽机的新时代

不锈钢的蒸汽机
满载着新阶层的创意驶进了新天地;

斯蒂芬·孙操作着手柄,
扭转,推敲,
铲出黑粉末灌进网杯,
锁紧,打开蒸汽旋塞……

端起温过的陶瓷杯,
萃取咖啡,
煤炭色浓缩汁滴入一个白色小瓷杯;

准备好钢壶,
再次打开蒸汽阀门,调压,
蒸汽的嘶嘶声植入进了牛奶中;

注入杯中摆上茶勺
比例完美的
一杯卡布奇诺,
正聚集着能量的动力……

困惑的上海清晨如同经历了 "东方快车谋杀案"
直到喝了这杯浓咖啡。

AA & CP

乔治·斯蒂芬森 (1781-1848) 设计建造了早期的蒸汽机车。作者以"斯蒂芬森"虚构冠名给做咖啡的师傅就是想借用早期蒸汽机车比喻当年上海咖啡馆用的蒸汽咖啡机。

The pig truck, Beijing

After dark the pig truck comes by, stinking and snorting, edging blackly into the hotel courtyard close to midnight. Secretary Wang and his foreign guests are full, Banker Zhang and his friends in the Ministry are done, Manager Liu and his secret mistress can't finish; Farmer Li gets buckets of leftovers from the stained tables. He pours the slops into a great black sludge in the hungry belly of the pig truck; and when it's gorged and full he cranks the donkey engine and it belches and farts its way back beyond the ever-wider megacity to feed the other model pigs.

北京的饲料车

饲料车在天黑之后开动,
哼哧着,臭味弥漫的
黑影,缓缓驶入
临近午夜的饭店后院。
王书记和他的
外国客人已经饱了,
银行家张先生和他的
政界朋友也吃好了,
刘经理和他的
情妇更是吃不下了。
农民老李从油渍渍的桌上
收了几桶剩菜,
倒进饲料车上
饥肠辘辘的
黑如泥浆的洞里。
狼吞虎咽
饱餐一顿之后
发动机的声音响起
打着饱嗝,放着臭屁
驶出这贪婪地
扩张中的大都市
回到农村
去喂其他的
纯正的猪。

HW & AR

Three ways

Confucius taught
a way of *should*:
The King should be kingly,
the subject, subject…

The rulers lapped it up; it was taught in every school

Laozi taught
a way of *is*:
Nothing is but hollow,
everything is from nothing being done…

Mystics breathed it in high among the mountain mists

Han Fei taught a
a way of *can*:
The people are but putty
for rewards and punishments…

The clever Kings, the sharp Generals, drove it forward

So Confucius stands revered millennia later because
we crave ideals;
And each generation finds Laozi as a way of healing;

But Han Fei the cynic?
Never disappointed. Never surprised. Practiced everywhere.

三种道路

孔子教导
应该的路：
做君要像君，
做臣要像臣……

虽历经改朝换代；所有学校仍在传教此道

老子倡导
存在的路：
天下万物生於有，
有生於无……

此道被深山隐士们极力推崇并发扬光大

韩非训导
能够的路：
君主制服臣下的权柄
重赏严罚……

精明的君王严苛的将领更将此言推崇至上

于是千百年来孔子之说被尊崇传承
因我们仍旧渴求理想典范；
世代也均有人凭老子之道找到慰籍；

然而愤世嫉俗的韩非又如何呢？
绝不会对其失望。亦不会对其惊诧。普天下实行着罢了。

AA & CP

Paul Lin at TopCom

Paul Lin at TopCom would fix everything:
The brass plate amongst the twenty or so by
the steep narrow stairs of the crappy building
said, 'Import/Export' – anything that moved.
'You wan' LCD screen? DRAM? Disk drive?
I get you Sharp, Casio, Panasonic,
Toshiba? Which one you wan'?
I got GMP, US Mil-Spec. Can do surface-mount.
Make for GE, Honeywell, everybody happy.'

He fixed an introduction to Seiko-Epson;
in Osaka we got into technical discussion –
A smaller screen with connectors on the side?
But we couldn't order volume so, nothing doing;
the prototype stagnated for another year –
an algorithm on a lap-top with spaghetti wires
to a mock-up of bits cannibalised from a
Casio calculator. Hand-held? Not yet. Not till
Paul Lin called in some post-dated cheques.

顶电有限公司的林保罗

顶电有限公司的林保罗精明强干：
拥挤的办公楼，狭窄的楼梯间
挂着二十多个公司的招牌，其中就有
顶电有限公司，"电器进出口"—— 全能通用
"你要液晶屏？动态随机存取存储器？优盘存储器？
我有夏普、卡西欧、松下、
东芝。你要哪一种品牌，啊？
我有良好生产规范，美国军用版部件。可直接贴装在电路板。
霍尼韦尔公司和通用电气都是我的客户，全部好评。"

他安排我们与精工爱普生合作；
为商讨设计修改我们抵达大阪——
需要更小型的屏幕还有侧面连接器？
因资金不足无法批量购件，无法协商；
原型设备的测试不得不延续一年——
手提电脑上的编码由经像意大利面条的线路
传到模拟的由卡西欧计算器替代的屏幕
为设备测试。手持式？还未达到。最后还是
林保罗从欠款的客户中为我们找到了供货商。

AA & CP

Tiananmen

The fundamentalists in History decided
'Oriental' was no longer kosher
so the Department was renamed
'East Asian Studies' and moved to 'Arts South',
two square towers with a bridge between
resembling the fort gates of old Peking;
it was nicknamed 'Tiananmen'.

And in those heady days we
escaped from serious study there to
share confidences, idle away the afternoons,
watch the sun go down through
flagons of red and white. We struck
poses of the Great Dictator and
harangued those down below.

The place produced interpreters,
a clutch of diplomats, a brace of spies,
a couple of writers, one or two
scholars of distinction, some
literate business people, cloned itself with
countless language teachers, and a few…
well, no-one knows…

And year in, year out they took us
through texts and orals and we learned:

Sense is something hard-won after
hours of not finding it in a dictionary.
Culture is a coarse homespun that takes the skin off.
Every object, every action, every property
has character… And civilisation
doesn't grow out of the barrel of a gun.

天安门

历史系的基要派们决定
"东方"一词不再圣洁
于是院系改名为"亚洲研究"
搬到了"人文南楼"——
一座桥架起两座钟楼,
像老北京的城门;
从此别名"天安门"。

在那不羁的日子里
我们从沉重的学业中逃离
到此分享秘密,共度光阴
看太阳徐徐落下
穿过一壶壶红白葡萄酒。
我们作出独裁者的姿态
高声批判楼下的行人。

这里培育出了几位翻译家,
一群外交官,一对间谍
一些作家,
一两个优秀学者,
几个有知识的商人,还克隆出
无数个中文教师,还有些嘛……
无人知晓。

年复一年,从课本上
讲堂上,我们领悟到:

理智来之不易,
无法在字典里苦苦寻得。
文化是粗糙的土布,能剥下一层皮。
每一个物体,每一个行为,每一个事件,
都有意义……而枪杆子里
出不了文明。

HW & AR

'Uraly'

for Stephen Lee

'"Uraly'? What is "uraly"?'
coaching kids for the
Nanjing Radio English Speech,
"juːʒʊəli…ˈjuːʒʊəli…the sound is "333"!
You'll send me mad!'

Grandson of Hong Kong's
pawn king millionaire,
sent away by your film star mother;
she feared you'd amount to nothing
surrounded by all that…

And fifty years ago,
teaching Chinese,
youthful, dynamic, always at a run,
demanding only the best from us.

On your bookshelves,
a row of eggshell opera masks,
the *China Pictorial* with its
rosy-cheeked workers,
Legge's richly bound *Chinese Classics* –
the school was your life.

Now here in a single room at the
Nanwai teachers' hostel –
golden silk shirts and mystery godson,
utterly uncompromising –
a billion things to fix.

'Uraly'

赠李祯顯

"'Uraly'？什么是'uraly'？"
南京广播英语演讲比赛上
教训着孩子们
"'juːʒʊəli……'juːʒʊəli…… 发音是ʒʒʒ!
你们要把我逼疯了！"

身家百万的祖父
香港典当行大亨，
你从小被影星母亲送出国；
她担心你在那样的环境下
将一无所成……

五十年前，中文课上
你风华正茂，神采奕奕
总是雷厉风行
要求我们做到最好……

在你的书架上
排列着如蛋壳般的京剧脸谱；
《人民画报》的封面
工人们红彤彤的面庞；
理雅各翻译的《中国经典》全集——
你的生活总是离不开学校。

如今在这里，
南外教师的单人公寓
你穿着金丝衬衫，带着身份神秘的教子——
仍不妥协，继续纠正
数不清的错误。

HW & AR

Miss Qu takes Entrepreneurship

One name on the class list grabs my attention:
Scion of the High Lord Gao Yang…

China does that – the 'Hundred Names'…
Sooner or later
everyone's descended from someone famous.

So we start class and get to the
Business Model Canvas
because this is where we are today…
And she must be so tired of being asked,
'Aren't you…?'

But my concentration flakes –
I am sick and sad at heart and stand irresolute…

– to a young man
glossing songs from dictionaries
in a run-down rented house, marriage failing…

Because I know what happened:
His hopes. His exile. His desperation –
I take my fashion from the good men of old:
A garb unlike the one the rude world cares for…

I've read it. All of it. Every word.

But we stay on track,
this generation so young and smart;
there are jobs to be done and we must focus on the topic:
crowd-funding for a new model of aged care in China…

Ha! He too was in his 60s
when he filled his gown with sand…

屈同学上创业管理课

名单上的一个名字吸引了我的注意：
　　　　帝高陽之苗裔兮……

中国就是如此——
百家姓，或早或晚
大家都会是名人的后裔。

于是我们开始上课
讲到"商业模式画布"
因为这是今天的主题。
我想她一定也听够了
　"难道你是……？"

而我的思绪开始游离
　　　　忳鬱邑余侘傺兮……

一个年轻男子
埋首书本，钻研诗词。
在破败的出租屋里，面临着即将衰亡的婚姻……

我知道那时发生了什么：
他的希冀。他的流亡。他的绝望——
　　　　謇吾法夫前修兮
　　　　非世俗之所服……

每一字，每一句，我都读过了。

但现在我们还得继续，
这一代人如此年轻，如此聪颖，
还有许多未完成的任务，我们必须专注：
"中国养老的众筹模式"……

哈！他那时也年近古稀
在长袍里装满了沙石……

Fragrance and richness mingled in sweet confusion;
the brightness of their lustre has remained undimmed…

And somehow we get through to the last lecture on
Net Present Value
with his voice still singing softly at my shoulder:
How can I live with men whose hearts are strangers to me?
I am going on a far journey to be away from them…
Long was the road that lay ahead and full of difficulties…

Not sure how much longer I can do this.

芳與澤其雜糅兮
　　唯昭質其猶未虧……

终于我们捱到了最后一课
"净现值法则"
他的声音依然在我耳旁轻轻萦绕：
　　何離心之可同兮
　　吾將遠逝以自疏
　　路修遠以多難兮……

不知我还能坚持多久。

HW & AR

Members of the China Cabinet

Alice Ayres has lived in many places, most recently in England, Germany and Japan. Alice was named after Lewis Carroll's heroine and likes to believe in impossible things. As a lawyer, this is not always easy.

He Wenhui was born in China and came to Australia when she was seventeen. She studied Fine Arts in Sydney and is currently studying for a Master of Interpreting and Translation Studies at Monash University in Melbourne.

Connie Pan has been a dedicated librarian and translator for the past thirty years. Connie is an avid reader of both Chinese and English literature. She particularly enjoys reading the same novel twice, in both languages.

Annie Ren is a translator and a PhD scholar at the Australian National University. She is the Chinese translator of Brian Castro and John Young's trilingual book *Macau Days*, published by Arts + Australia.

Painter and calligrapher Paul Hsiu Pa Yang was born in Beijing in 1925. He worked in the Chinese section of the BBC's Overseas Service and taught Chinese in the School of Oriental and African Studies at London University, afterwards migrating to Australia, where he joined the Chinese Section of the ABC and taught at the University of Melbourne.

Christopher Nailer is a Canberra-based poet. He started studying Chinese with Stephen Lee at Camberwell Grammar School in 1964 and continued at the University of Melbourne. He wrote a Master's thesis on Qu Yuan in 1980. This is his fourth collection of poetry; it follows *Blundstones and a Brown Dog* (Ginninderra Press, 2006), *Peel Street* (Ginninderra Press, 2010) and *Travels with a Grand Piano* (Cyder Press, 2019).

www.ingramcontent.com/pod-product-compliance
Lightning Source LLC
Chambersburg PA
CBHW040527120526
44589CB00050B/2795